NATIVE AMERICANS

Created by Gallimard Jeunesse,
Ute Fuhr, and Raoul Sautai
Illustrated by Ute Fuhr
and Raoul Sautai

A FIRST DISCOVERY BOOK

SCHOLASTIC INC.
New York Toronto London Auckland Sydney

Around 30,000 years ago, hunters from Asia crossed into North America.

In 1492 when Christopher
Columbus landed in the
Americas, he discovered Native
Americans already living there.

Hopi pueblo

Iroquois house
of elm and birch bark

Mandan house
of earth and mud

Native Americans from
the Northwest coast made
houses of cedar, which were
elaborately decorated.

Cedar posts were
carved to create
totem poles,
which often told the
history of families.

Log cabin of a
Canadian fur trapper

Western pioneer
sod house

Eastern schoolhouse
of rock and wood

While moving toward the western frontier,
the pioneers stopped at night and formed
a big circle of wagons to guard their livestock.

Plains Indians used to live in tepees.

Young men learned
how to use weapons
for hunting.

A tepee was made of poles
covered with buffalo skins.

Women boiled water over hot rocks.
Most cooking, however, was done outside.

Communication took many forms.

These rocks meant "go right."

This grass sign also meant "go right."

These sticks meant "go right and walk for four days."

The bravest warriors of a tribe wore headdresses made of eagle feathers.

Smoke signals could be seen from very far away.

Pawnee
headdress of
porcupine and
deer hair

Headdress
of the Sioux
Indians

Mandan
headdress
of a
medicine
man

Cheyenne headdress
made of
buffalo hide
and hair

For all Native American boys,
the first buffalo hunt was a big event.

Native Americans of the northern forest
hunted bears, beavers, and elks for food
and clothing.

When the snow was deep, hunting was made
possible with snowshoes.

In the spring, cowboys corralled
the roaming livestock to select the cows
that would feed the nation.

The young cows were branded
by their owners. This one was
trying to get away . . .

. . . but it was soon
lassoed by one of the cowboys.

In the West, the first towns were constructed in the river valleys and then along the railroad tracks.

The sheriff kept
order in the town.

The stagecoach
transported passengers,
baggage, newspapers, and mail.

Soldiers and traders moved into every area of the West. They built forts where Native Americans exchanged furs for supplies. Soon conflicts arose between the Native Americans and the soldiers.

This herd of horses hides . . .

Native Americans
entering a fort.

The army was there to protect settlers and gold miners,

who were actually trespassing on lands that belonged to the Native Americans.

Eventually the Native Americans were defeated and forced to sign peace treaties. The ritual smoking of the pipe, or calumet, often marked these occasions.

The soldiers and settlers
who followed forever
changed the
landscape . . .

. . . along with the world of Native Americans.

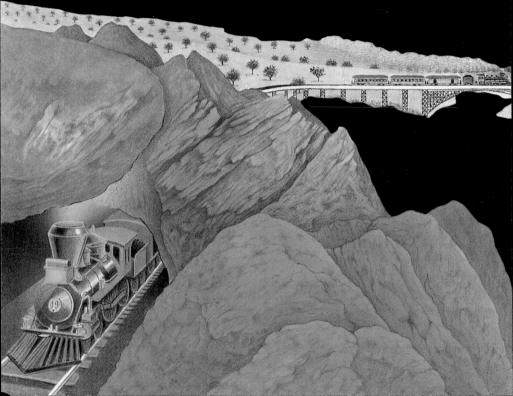

*Parents Magazine
"Best Books" Award

**Parenting Magazine
Reading Magic Award

***Oppenheim Toy Portfolio
Gold Seal Award

Library of Congress Cataloging-in-Publication Data available.

Originally published in France under the title *Les indiens* by Editions Gallimard Jeunesse.

ISBN 0-590-38153-9

Copyright © 1994 by Editions Gallimard Jeunesse.
This edition English translation by Heather Miller.
This edition American text by Wendy Barish.

12 11 10 9 8 7 6 5 4 3 2 1   8 9/9 0 1 2/0
Printed in Italy by Editoriale Libraria
First Scholastic printing, March 1998